Living Today

The Kitchen

3/6 ~~4/6~~

In the same series

Feeding the Family
Health and Care of the Family
Good Grooming and Clothes Care
Housing the Family
Decorating Your Home
Homemaking
The Family and the Social Services
Managing Your Money

Living Today   Book 8

The Kitchen

Margaret Cullen

Illustrated by Hilary Norman

Heinemann Educational Books. London

Heinemann Educational Books Ltd

LONDON EDINBURGH MELBOURNE AUCKLAND TORONTO
SINGAPORE HONG KONG KUALA LUMPUR
IBADAN NAIROBI JOHANNESBURG
LUSAKA NEW DELHI

ISBN 0435 42207 3

Designed by Design Practitioners Limited Sevenoaks

Published by Heinemann Educational Books Ltd
48 Charles Street, London WIX 8AH

Printed in Great Britain by Biddles Limited
Martyr Road, Guildford

Contents

Kitchen Planning

The Kitchen has always been the hub of the home but until recent times very little attention has been given to planning this room. The location of the kitchen—in relation to the rest of the home has varied at different times in history and in different parts of the world. At some periods it was usual for the only fire in the home to be in the living area so the cooking had to be carried out there. At other times the kitchen was in quite separate buildings from the main part of the house. Very little thought was put into the saving of labour in the kitchen. The table, sink and cupboards were put in the most space saving places but little thought was given to the amount of movement needed to run the kitchen.

Our basic equipment has been adapted from primitive devices first used centuries ago. Our means of cookery has always depended on the fuel available. Wood was used by the majority of people until the sixteenth century when coal was occasionally available. The rotisserie and the barbecue are modern versions of the oldest methods of cooking over an open fire. Pieces of food were skewered to twigs and held to the flames or glowing charcoal.

It was not until the twentieth century that kitchen design began to be considered worthy of study. While servants were cheap and willing to 'live in' few moves were made towards saving labour. But once the middle-class woman could no longer afford help in the home she refused to put up with the conditions she had considered good enough for her servants.

She demanded equipment to ease the burden of the work and insisted that the kitchen be reorganised so that she could do the essential work with the minimum of effort. The use of gas and electricity for cooking and lighting and the development of easily cleaned surfaces for equipment and work units has revolutionised work in the kitchen. This in turn led to a growing interest in planning and a thriving industry producing the equipment now regarded as essential.

Even with an unlimited amount of money to spend it would be impossible to plan a kitchen which would satisfy everyone. You can only plan your own ideal. However, no matter what type of kitchen you would like or how much money you have to spend you will still need to do a considerable amount of thinking, enquiring, and planning before making any final decisions or spending any money.

The kitchen can be one of the most expensive rooms to furnish. Many of the larger pieces of equipment are costly because they are made to last a number of years. This means that should you buy an unsuitable article it can be an expensive mistake which you may have to live with for a long time. The cost of labour to alter the position of fixtures needing mains supplies such as gas, electricity and water can be very high. It is sensible to make sure you do decide on the best position of these fixtures before any work is carried out.

It is easiest to plan a kitchen before the house is built but you rarely have the opportunity to do this. You may be able to alter the size and shape of the kitchen if you own the house but you are unlikely to be allowed to do this if you rent the property. Most people have to make the most of the existing shell of the kitchen. However, improvements can be made by rearranging the equipment and storage and by getting rid of useless furniture and equipment which merely clutters the kitchen.

The basic requirements are the same for every kitchen. 1 It should be attractive and comfortable to work in. 2 There should be sufficient equipment for the family needs and planned storage for this. 3 There should be a plentiful supply of hot water. 4 Provision should be made for as many labour saving devices as possible even if it will be some time before you can afford to purchase these. For example, power points for equipment you cannot yet afford should be included in your early plans. It will be less costly to have these fitted as part of an overall wiring system than to have to make additions later.

If you are to get the best value out of your kitchen you should list all the things you do, or plan to do, in your kitchen. The list will vary from one family to another but will include some of the following:
1 Preparation of food for meals 2 Preservation of food by jam making, bottling, freezing etc. 3 Serving meals in the kitchen 4 Laundry work 5 Needlework 6 Homework 7 Family hobbies 8 Flower arranging, shoe cleaning, etc.

Another list should include all the equipment you need for these activities. This could be subdivided into the essential items, the things you will need later, and the non-essentials which you might hope to have in the future even if they seem out of reach now. Costly items often become less expensive in time as the demand increases and technical improvements cut the cost of production.

You must work out how much money you can afford to spend. With sufficient money you can arrange most things to suit your own needs or employ an expert to do the job for you. Very few people can afford to do this. The less money you have to spare the more important is the need to plan your spending so that you get the best value for your money. You cannot afford to make mistakes.

You will need as much information as possible before spending any money. This will take time. Collect brochures and leaflets from manufacturers, shops and exhibitions. Read any books and magazines you can get on the subject. Note any points you find interesting or useful. Get the opinions of friends and relatives on the various appliances they have bought and if possible

ask them to let you try them out. Learn from other people's mistakes. It is less costly than learning from your own. You will probably find it necessary to work out a simple filing system to organise the information you have collected.

Make an outline plan of the existing kitchen on squared paper with as large a scale as possible. Stick this plan on to a sheet of cardboard. Mark in the existing pipes, doors, and windows, and show all measurements. You can refer to this whenever you wish to check space available rather than having to be constantly measuring in the kitchen itself.

If you intend to employ outside help to carry out structural alteration or decoration you should get estimates from several firms. These estimates should be detailed so that you know the exact charges for each item of work to be done and the quality of the materials to be used. Remember that should you change your mind over any particular item or want any extra work carried out you should ask for supplementary estimates. Budget for the fact that this will increase your final bill. The lowest tender for the work may not be the most economical. Study the estimates carefully before making a final decision.

If you do not know which builders in your area carry out such projects you could probably find out by making enquiries at the shops who supply kitchen units or by writing directly to the Master Builders Association. A number of firms specialise in kitchen reorganisation and will undertake all the work concerned from building and decorating to fitting all the equipment.

If you are doing any structural alterations to the house you may have to get permission for this from the local authority. Plans will have to be submitted to them for approval. Local by-laws vary so it is sensible to check on local regulations before starting on any major alterations. Should you break local by-laws in any way, such as by extending the house beyond the building line or by using a material considered unsuitable to the area, you could find yourself having to demolish the new structure.

Rented Houses or Flats

If you rent a house or flat there may be limits to the amount of alteration you may be allowed to make. You cannot knock down walls or get rid of any fittings you dislike without permission from the landlord. He might be co-operative and even be willing to help with the cost if he considers it will improve his property but is unlikely to do so otherwise. Check your agreements. Make sure you get written permission from the landlord before you make alterations of any sort. If you are carrying out an extensive scheme it might be as well to ask your solicitor to work out an agreement between you and your landlord. You will not wish to spend a lot of time and money on the property only to find your rent increased because of improved amenities.

If the kitchen units are not suitable for your needs you might be able to rearrange them, use them in the spare room for 'dead' storage or just store them in the attic or the garden shed. Do not dispose of them without the landlord's written consent. They are part of his property and should be replaced before you move out of the premises.

If you are paying for units and equipment yourself buy only such pieces that will be useful in your next home and which can be removed without damaging the house structure. If you intend to stay in the house or flat for only a short time you might find it worth-while to enquire about the cost of renting some of the more expensive items.

You have already listed all the possible uses of your kitchen. You must now consider all the various aspects of the kitchen itself which as a whole will allow you to carry out these activities.

1 The position and shape of the kitchen 2 The layout of the kitchen according to its usage 3 The choice of fittings, furnishings and storage 4 Lighting and power points 5 Flooring 6 Wall surfaces 7 Decoration

The Size and Shape of the Kitchen

This could vary from a tiny kitchenette to a large farmhouse type kitchen. A kitchen of 10-12 square metres is generally found to be the most useful for a family of 4 or 5 people. Many houses are now being built with just one living room and a kitchen rather than the traditional two living rooms in order to allow for a larger kitchen. While the majority of people complain that their kitchens are too small those with really large kitchens can also have problems. Unless the working areas and equipment are grouped carefully there is the problem of having to move about far more than is necessary in order to carry out each task. In this case it is as well to concentrate the working area along adjoining walls facing a corner or to divide the kitchen up into definite work areas for cooking, laundry work, eating etc. It might even be sensible to separate each working area by making partitions of storage units, sliding partitions, blinds or climbing plants.

If the kitchen is very small, equipment must be kept to a minimum and every part of the room must be used to the full. If it is possible equipment and small utensils which are not in regular use may be stored elsewhere in the house. It may be possible to arrange for the bathroom to be used for laundry work, for the cleaning cupboard to be put elsewhere in the house. The kitchen is not the best place for laundry work or the cleaning cupboard even if it is a large room and the hygienic hazards are increased if the space is limited.

Ideally the kitchen should be near the dining room and hall and have access to the garden for the disposal of refuse, to be near the clothes line and the herb, vegetable and front gardens. The north side of the house will be coolest so this is the best position for a larder.

Work Areas

The equipment must be laid out in such a way as to make the best use of the space available and to allow for every task to be carried out with the minimum of physical effort and in the shortest time. Every task has a natural sequence of movement and the equipment should be placed with reference to this sequence.

The sequence for preparing food is storage of food, preparation, cooking, and serving. The work areas of this sequence are a preparation surface, sink and cooker. These should be arranged so that the walking distance is kept to the minimum and never exceed 2 metres. There should be a working surface on either side of the sink and cooker so that there is plenty of space to put things down. Where ever possible the working surfaces should link the sink and cooker thus:

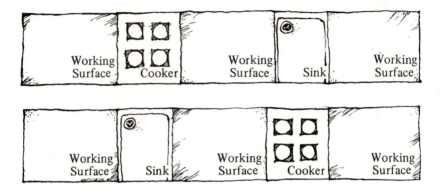

Working surfaces each side of the cooker will take care of the problem of projecting pan handles.

The oven part of the cooker need not be included in this working sequence as a dish to be baked or roasted is usually more or less completed once it is ready to be put in the oven. A working surface next to the oven will help when you are taking out hot dishes. Breaks in the flow of this work sequence are often the cause of accidents. Do not put an oven right next to a doorway as there is a danger of collision at times when you are holding hot utensils. Draughts could blow out the flame of gas appliances and could lower the temperature of an open oven. If the doorway is seldom used and not really needed it might be worth blocking the doorway temporarily with storage cupboards or permanently with a built-in wall. Such a door from the dining room could be blocked in, up to working height and have a serving hatch fitted from this level. Low level equipment such as refrigerators, washing machines and dishwashers, could all be sited under an unbroken working surface.

The four basic layouts are:

1 *The galley* where a long narrow kitchen is fitted on two sides with working units. There is very little distance between the two rows, most of the walking involves doubling up and down the length of the kitchen.

2 *The L shaped layout.* Here the units are grouped along two adjoining walls. This is an efficient plan for a large kitchen. A table could be put into the remaining corner.

3 *The U shaped layout* has equipment down two opposite walls and along the connecting wall. The remaining wall is left free for the door and a table.

4 *A divided layout* with one area of the kitchen planned for cooking and the dining area separated by a waist high unit or similar partition. This is useful for the mother of young children who can play in the dining area under her supervision but are safe from the hazards of the working area.

Galley

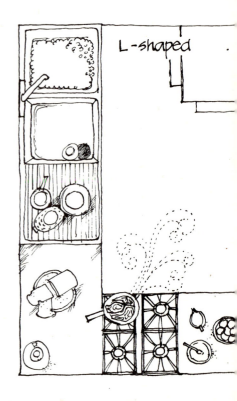

L-shaped

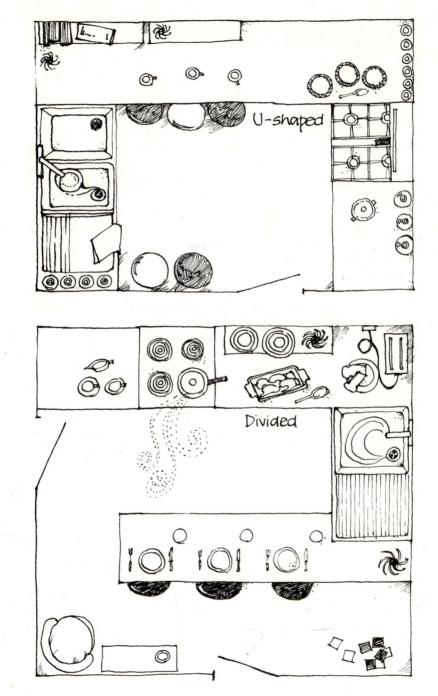

U-shaped

Divided

In existing kitchens it is not always possible to adhere completely to a basic layout. It may be necessary to compromise to make the best use of the existing space and equipment.

It is widely recognised that awkward working heights are the cause of many ailments and accidents. People vary in height and length of arm. As a result most manufacturers make their units to suit the woman of average height 1.63m so that women who are many centimetres shorter or taller than this may find the average unit uncomfortable to work at for any length of time. A few manufacturers are concerned about this and are producing units which can be varied in height by using different sized base plinths or by suspending them from adjustable wall brackets. It is easy to work out the best working height for an individual. She should be wearing the kind of shoes most suitable for working in the kitchen. She should stand up straight with arms at the sides but the hands stretched flat parallel to the floor. The distance between the floor and the flat of the hand is the best height for most jobs. For sitting down jobs the working height should be 12 centimetres less. For some jobs there should be a slightly higher working surface. Most kitchens are used by more than one person. It would be impossible to suit them all. The best compromise would be to have the main work area to suit the one who works most in the kitchen and to provide areas of work surface at different heights for the infrequent use of others. These could be in the form of a table, a divider base unit or a refrigerator top. A continuous run of working surface does not necessarily have to be at the same height throughout its length.

Some cookers can be obtained at various heights. If they are to be built in to form a continuous working surface they will have to be lower than the standard free-standing models. This problem does not arise with split level cookers as the range and oven can be fitted to any height you choose.

Base units are usually made of standard depths of 35, 52 and 60 cms. Plumbing, gas and electrical connections need to be fitted behind some of the units. In order to keep the fronts of the units in line it should be possible to combine deep and shallow units so that the connections are accommodated in spaces behind shallow units. A single working surface can cover the whole area, bridging the cavities so that the units appear to be of uniform size. Many of the new cookers, dishwashing and automatic washing machines are deeper than most units but these could be lined up in a similar way leaving a cavity under the back of the working surface. Remember to fill in the gap at the side of the end unit as otherwise it would be almost impossible to remove any dirt blown through it to the back of the units.

Work surfaces should be made of a hard easily cleaned material. At the present time plastic laminates are the most popular materials for this purpose. You could have a section of wood inserted into this working surface for a permanent chopping board, marble for rolling pastry and stainless steel on either side of the cooking range. In this case care must be taken for all joins to be filled in and carefully sealed otherwise they become dirt traps.

The Sink
The sink is in constant use so should be of a very durable material. It can be made of stainless steel, enamelled steel, fibreglass, plastic or fireclay. It may be formed as part of a unit moulded in one piece with the draining board or sunk into a work surface.

The sink should be large enough for family use. A double sink unit is ideal but if the space would only allow two very small sinks it would be better to choose a single large sink. You can get several different arrangements of sinks such as one large and one small or two large and one very small for cutlery and vegetable preparation. Study the manufacturers brochures to find out the latest arrangements available. For the average woman the convenient depth of a sink for most purposes is between 17 and 22 cms with the top rim at working height.

Most sinks are available with a choice of two sizes of drain outlet, the standard size and the larger one which would, if necessary, take a waste disposal unit. Most, but not all sinks, are fitted with an overflow. This is almost an essential fitting as there is certain to be a time when someone will forget to turn off a tap and, if the outlet is plugged, the result could be a flooded kitchen.

Where space permits it is useful to have a double draining board. If these are not moulded as one with the sink they should be removeable for cleaning. The draining board must be fitted at the correct angle so that the water drains into the sink not on to the floor or down the wall. You can choose between ribbed or smooth draining boards. Ribbed boards drain more efficiently but a flat one can provide an extra working surface.

Clean the sink and draining board each time after use. Never use harsh cleansers which may damage the surface. A mild paste cleanser will remove stains from most surfaces. For special cleaning follow the instructions for the care of the material from which the sink is made.

Kitchen Floors

The floor should be comfortable to walk on, hard wearing, waterproof and resistant to household acids, alkali, grease and heat. It should be easy to clean, nonslip when wet or dry, and warm with a certain amount of resilience. The ideal kitchen flooring has yet to be invented but a good quality vinyl meets most conditions except extreme heat. Vinyl covered cork combines the attractive appearance, warmth and resilience of cork with the easy-care surface of vinyl. Cork and vinyl are obtainable in a range of attractive colours.

Other floor coverings include rubber, linoleum, ceramic tile, brick, flagstone, slate and terrazzo but the drawbacks of these range from being slippery when wet to lack of resilience and high cost.

Walls and Ceilings

The wall behind work surfaces and sink should have a splash proof surface at least 30 centimetres high. This should be of a tough material which can withstand the wear of water, household acids and alkali, and grease. Most of the materials suitable for work tops can be used as well as ceramic, glass or steel tiles, or sheets of vinyl, steel glass or plastic faced hardboard. Other walls need not be so tough but must be easy to clean. They could be covered with plastic coated wallpaper or fabric, several coats of matt or semi-gloss paint, panels of plastic laminate or decorative wood treated with a clear plastic seal. If you should

choose to use wood for such a purpose remember that it should
be fireproofed first.

Ceilings can be covered with sound-absorbent acoustic tiles, translucent plastic sheets or several coats of emulsion paint. It should be easily cleaned and resistant to condensation.

Curtains and Blinds

If the window is near a water heater or cooker a blind should be fitted rather than a curtain which could easily be blown over the appliance and catch fire. A venetian or roller blind would be suitable. Both are available in a wide range of colours and sizes. You can save money by buying blind kits and making your own. Roller blinds and curtains should be made of washable materials which stand up to the steam heat and grease to be found in the kitchen. Cottons, fibreglass fabric and plastic coated cottons are all easily cared for and hardwearing.

Colour in the Kitchen

Plastic laminate surfaced units and large pieces of equipment such as refrigerators and stoves are expensive and should last a long time. Choose a basic colour for these that will still be as pleasing to you in many years time. You can buy these items in many colours but white will probably remain the favoured choice because it is liked by the majority of people, and can be teamed with so many colours. This may seem rather lacking in courage or adventure but few people can buy new equipment when they tire of the colour. You can get plenty of colour into your scheme with the things that are inexpensive to replace. Curtains, painted shelves, cushions on stools as well as colourful inexpensive pottery, posters on the wall, teacloths and storage tins all allow for inexpensive experiments in the use of colour. Colours do go out of fashion in home decorating as well as in clothing.

Lighting

A kitchen needs good general lighting, bright lighting over work tops, cupboard lighting and lights in ovens and refrigerations. In a dark room natural light may need constant supplementing with artificial light. A kitchen decorated in dark colours will need more lighting than one decorated in light colours. Fluorescent strip lighting is suitable for the kitchen because of its 'no shadow' qualities. For work-top lighting strip-lights can be fitted under the fronts of the wall cabinets so that the light shines down on the work you are doing. Spot lights can be directed down on to cooking ranges or tables. Automatic interior lights can be fitted to light up when cupboard doors are opened.

The Hot Water Supply
A plentiful supply of hot water to the kitchen is essential. The amount of hot water needed in different households varies considerably. Normally about 45 litres of hot water is used each day at the sink, except where there is a dishwasher. Hot water may be supplied from the main household supply by sink water heaters. If the length of pipe from the hot water heater to the kitchen tap exceeds 8 metres the wastage of the heat from the pipe could be high. In this case a sink water heater would probably save money. This should be large enough to supply sufficient hot water for kitchen needs. The very small models giving off about 2 litres of hot water a minute are ideal for handbasins but far too slow for the kitchen sink.

Electric water heaters These must be connected to the cold water supply and to a 13 amp power point. The kind that fits into the end of a cold tap is considered dangerous because should the electrodes come into contact with the water both the water and the piping will become 'live'. Electric water heaters should always be connected by a qualified electrician. Faulty electrical connections used with water could cause severe or even fatal electric shocks. Most electric water heaters are thermostatically controlled to prevent wastage of electricity. There are several types of water heaters suitable for installation in the kitchen.

Single point water heaters are available in several sizes. They can be fixed onto the wall above the sink so that the spout at the bottom of the tank can supply water directly to the sink. If there is no space above the sink because of windows or cupboards the heater can be fitted underneath. In this case a special mixer tap will be needed. If the heater is connected to the cold water main the hot water from it is as suitable for cooking as water boiled in a kettle.

Multipoint water heaters will supply sufficient hot water for all household needs. They can be wall mounted, fitted under the sink or in a cupboard. The dual purpose pressure type heater has two heating elements. The upper element keeps 23-35 litres of hot water ready for instant use at the sink or hand basin. The lower element is switched on to heat the whole contents of the water cistern when it is needed for bathing, cleaning and laundry work. Connection is to the supply from the household cistern. If the water is to be used for cooking the cistern must be kept covered and checked regularly for rusting and corrosion.

Cistern type water heaters may be fitted above the level of the highest tap in the house. This heater can be connected directly to the cold water main and no separate cold water cistern is needed. These are useful where space is too limited for the fitting of a multipoint heater.

There is a simple water heater which does not have to be connected to the water supply and can be heated from a convenient 13 amp power plug. It consist of a small water tank with a tap fixed to the wall above the sink. It is filled with water by means of a hose from the cold water tap. Basically this is just like heating water in a large electric kettle but an electric kettle holding this amount of water would be very heavy to lift.

Gas water heaters These may be linked to the central heating system or may be the instantaneous type where the water is heated by being passed over the burners before being delivered to the tap. Most gas heaters must have a vent through the outside wall to get rid of fumes. Most models have temperature controls. Some have push button ignition. The water heater may be fitted to the wall near the sink and connected to the cold water and gas pipes. If this is not convenient it may be fitted next to the hot water cylinder.

Ventilation

Good ventilation is essential in every room for the comfort, health and efficiency of the occupants. It is especially important in the kitchen because of the steam, cooking odours and excessive heat that are liable to collect there. The ventilation should remove the stale air and replace it with fresh without creating a draught or wasting the heating fuel.

In some kitchens natural ventilation through doors, windows and chimneys might be sufficient. The stove should be positioned in the path of the air currents passing from an inner door to the open windows. This is seldom sufficient to combat the problem in a kitchen where a lot of cooking is done. In this case it would be sensible to fit a ventilator. This would prove less expensive than having to redecorate frequently because of the damage caused by condensation.

The most popular mechanical types of ventilation include louvred windows, moveable valves let into window panes and wedge shaped vents set high in the wall. If the louvred window is a fairly large one make sure it is fitted with a locking device so that the louvre cannot be removed from the outside allowing access to burglars as well as air!

Even this type of ventilation might be insufficient. Electrical extraction fans may be needed. These are available in several sizes and are designed for either drawing air into the room or for extracting it. Running speeds can be fixed or made variable. A model fitted with a shutter which automatically closes when the extractor is switched off will prevent the problem of draughts coming back through the vent. After the initial fitting the fan needs little attention beyond occasional dusting and for some models, very infrequent oiling. The fan must be positioned so that air is drawn away from the rest of the house and so that steam and kitchen odours are not directed into other rooms, the air should pass over the cooker on the way to the ventilator.

A ductless hood fitted above the cooker will remove grease, smoke, steam and odours from the air. The air is drawn in by an electric fan, passed through a grease filter and a layer of activated charcoal and then the clean warm air passes back into the kitchen. The charcoal will need renewing at intervals.

Waste Disposal

It is convenient to have a small rubbish bin in the kitchen. There are numerous bins designed for kitchen use. Make sure you choose one of a suitable size. It should be emptied daily and kept clean and dry. A foot-operated opening device cuts down the need for touching the bin with the hands. There are several types available which are basically specially made holders for plastic or paper bags. When the bag is full it is discarded with its contents and a new bag put into place. It is a good idea to tie up the top of the discarded full bag with string or an elastic band or to staple it shut. Several models are available which heat seals the filled plastic bag with an electric device incorporated in the holder.

Every household needs at least one dustbin. In some areas these are provided by the local authority. They may be made of galvanised metal, plastic, rubber or resin impregnated paper. If the dustbin is used for the disposal of hot ashes you need a metal bin but choose a rubber lid or one with a rubber edge as this is quieter in use than a metal lid. If you collect a lot of refuse it is sensible to have several small bins rather than one very large bin as this would be very heavy when full.

The Refuse Bin

1 It should have a well fitted lid to keep out flies and rodents.
2 The bin should be kept as clean as possible. The paper sack variety is the most hygienic as the sack is disposed of with the rubbish and replaced by a new one. Other types should be washed out and disinfected regularly. Keep it as dry as possible.
3 Rinse out bottles, tins and jars before disposing of them. Drain food waste and other wet garbage as dry as possible and wrap it up well in paper before putting it in the bin.
4 Outside bins should be kept as far from the kitchen as reasonably possible. Choose a well-ventilated place out of the sunlight. Metal bins should be stood on bricks so that the air can circulate around the base and keep it dry. This will help prevent rusting.

5 Make sure the bin is accessible to the dustman for collection. If you have to carry a bin any distance arrange for help or have a simple trolley made.

Many local councils salvage certain refuse such as metals or paper. Should this apply to your area you should keep these materials separate from other rubbish. The council sells the salvage and this helps keep down the local rates.

Storage

Apart from cooking, work, which starts or ends up in the kitchen, may include cleaning and washing and ironing. All these operations require equipment and it must have storage. Storage must be planned for food and drinks, crockery, pots and pans, kitchen tools, cleaning and laundry materials and equipment. These take up a great deal of space. Each year more equipment becomes available and within the means of the average family. When you first plan your kitchen you should bear this in mind and try to allow sufficient storage for future purchases even if this seems in excess of present needs. There is no need to purchase the extra storage units now but they should be put into the plan so that there is space for them when they are needed.

All cupboards should be simply designed with adequate shelving and easy to clean surfaces of laminated plastic or enamel paint. Drawers should run easily and be the right size to take your equipment. Wall cupboard doors should open through 120° minimum. Sliding doors of units should run smoothly and be easily removed to facilitate special cleaning of the storage space. There should not be awkward dirt-collecting corners. Base units and cupboards should have a toe recess at floor level to prevent stubbed toes and scuffed units. Any high units projecting from the wall are best carried up to ceiling height. This will prevent dirt and dust collecting on the top and provide additional storage for articles which are seldom used but must be kept. Wall cupboards above working surfaces must be carefully positioned if they are not to get in the way. They should be at least 45 cms above the working surface and even higher if they are very deep.

Arrange your storage so that everything is stored as near as possible to the place where it will be used. This is especially important for things in constant use. The contents of storage units should be readily visible and accessible. Shelves should be adjustable to meet changing needs.

Food Storage

In some areas local bye-laws require a new dwelling to have a larder and usually require that it should be ventilated to the outside air. In homes where there is a refrigerator of reasonable size the larder is of declining importance so long as there is a cool place for the storage of vegetables and perishable foods which are not to be stored in the refrigerator. It is usually possible to provide a cool cupboard for this purpose.

The facilities for food storage will vary with the size of the kitchen, the needs of the family and the amount of money available for equipment. (Refrigerators and deep freezers are discussed in detail in Chapter 3.) A cool larder is ideal but a kitchen cupboard may be substituted. Shelves should be of easily cleaned material with a sealed surface where dirt cannot lodge. Plastic laminates are efficient and extremely durable. Less permanent but effective seals are thin adhesive plastics film or gloss paint. Walls and floors should also be of an easily cleaned material. Air vents should be covered with flyproof metal gauze.

2 The Cooker

The cooker heads the list of essential kitchen equipment. Most people must expect to keep a cooker for a long time before replacing it with a newer model. The cooker is used several times a day and is on view all the time. It should not be an 'impulse' purchase.

Cooking methods changed very little from the earliest times right up to the eighteenth century. Until then cooking was done over an open fire or in a brick oven. In the eighteenth century ranges were introduced. They were heated first by wood and later by coal. It took a lot of energy to keep these ranges supplied with fuel and to keep them clean and blackleaded. The first gas cookers were on show at the Exhibition of 1851 but they were not generally used for at least fifty years. The electric cooker was brought out at the end of the century but was not widely used until the 1930's. The early gas and electric stoves were great improvements on the kitchen ranges in that they did not need constant refuelling. They were constructed in similar materials to the ranges and needed to be cleaned in the same way.

Most people now use gas or electricity although solid fuel and oil cookers are available. Modern stoves are easy to control and

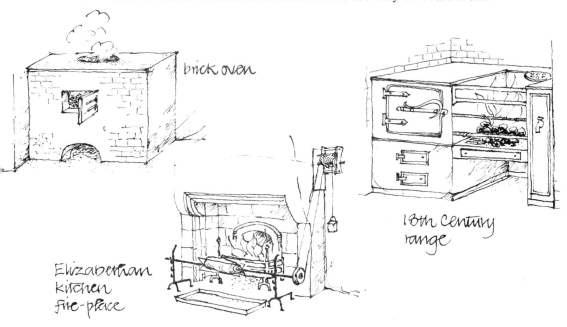

brick oven

18th Century range

Elizabethan kitchen fire-place

to clean. Whichever type of heat source you choose there are various things you must consider before making your purchase.

1 If you use more gas appliances than electric ones in your home you should be buying your gas at a cheap rate so that it is economical to have a gas cooker. If on the other hand you use mainly electrical appliances it would be sensible to choose an electrical stove. It is extravagant to pay standing charges just for the use of a gas stove. If you want an appliance which will give continuous cooking facilities plus a constant supply of hot water a solid fuel or oil fired heat storage cooker might be more suitable.

2 Consider the cost of the cooker. Is it within the price range you can afford? If you are using a hire purchase scheme make sure you can afford the repayments. Remember to find out the cost of installation. If you are buying a new house it may be possible to have a built-in split-level cooker included on the mortgage. It is sensible to purchase the largest cooker you can afford which will fit into the kitchen. Optional features can help to improve cooking but they add a lot to the cost of the cooker. Make sure you only purchase extras which will be of use to you.

early gas cooker

heat storage cooker

3 The stove should be designed to be easy to clean. Bright chromium plate looks attractive but if decorative pieces are also dirt traps they will soon become a nuisance. Many stoves are made with a non-stick surface which resists dirt. Others are made with oven linings which can be removed for cleaning. There are several ovens which are self cleaning. Whenever possible choose a cooker which has no gap between it and the floor. Cookers are heavy to move and in any case can only be moved a short distance.

4 Check for safety. Controls, especially for gas stoves, should be out of reach of young children. Make sure there are no sharp projections. Find out if you can purchase a safety device to hold saucepans in position. Controls should be easily reached when the hotplates are in use without the risk of scalding from steam. Handles should be of a material which does not overheat when the cooker is in use.

5 Make sure the cooker will fit into your kitchen. Measure the width and height of the space available. If the kitchen is narrow make sure there is space to open the oven door. Remember that you must allow for space behind a gas cooker for the pipes. You can now purchase top cooker and split level cookers. Hobs can be inserted into working tops. If you wish you can have gas hobs with electric ovens or vice versa. These can be fitted at opposite ends of the room if this should suit your kitchen plan.

The standard cooker consists of an oven, a grill and a hob with several boiling rings or burners. These sections are arranged in a variety of ways.

1 The cooker can have a hob top with the grill beneath it, both fitted on to the top of the oven.

2 The grill can be at eye level fixed to the splash back above the hob or be a completely separate unit.

3 Double width cookers may have one very large oven, two ordinary sized ovens or one large plus one small oven and a warming cupboard. The grill can be under the hob, at eye level or in one of the ovens.

4 Split level cookers are useful as they allow for flexibility in kitchen planning. The hob top is at working height set into a

counter or table top. The oven may be set at a suitable height elsewhere in the kitchen. Many manufacturers of kitchen furniture make housing units for these items. If you wish you can choose a hob of one make and the oven of another.

Ovens may be opened from right or left or have a drop down door. The door may have a glass inset or there may be a second inner door made of glass. Many ovens have a light inside controlled by the door or by a light switch. All ovens have two or three shelves and five or six runner positions. Optional extras may include clocks, automatic timers, rotisserie spits, thermostatic plates or burners, roastmeters, non-stick oven linings, automatic oven cleaning, lights in oven and above hotplate.

Automatic Cooking in Gas and Electric Ovens

Automatic cooking frees the cook from having to attend to the oven once she has prepared the food. Automatic timing can be used for complete meals, dishes cooked separately or overnight cooking. It is convenient to be able to put the dishes for breakfast in the oven and to find them cooked ready for you when you get up in the morning. You can be away for the whole day or part of the day and have a hot meal as soon as you return home. Should you be delayed the meal will not be burnt. Dishes which take a long time to cook such as large turkeys or rich fruit cakes can be cooked overnight. All automatic cookers can be used on a manual setting as an ordinary cooker. It is a good idea to get to know the characteristics of your own cooker before using the automatic controls. Cookers, even of the same make, do vary slightly in the speed in which they cook and brown food and in the temperature variations of different parts of the oven. When you have got used to your cooker, read the relevant section in the instruction book and experiment with the automatic controls. At first it is a good idea to cook one or two meals while you are going to be around to correct any minor mistakes. This will reassure you that you have learnt to use the controls correctly and that the heat is really turned on and off at the times you have chosen.

Electric Cookers

The electric cooker is flameless and the element gives off
nothing but heat so this is a very clean method of cooking.
Until recently each part of the cooker was controlled by a three
or four heat switch. Now all the hotplates have multiheat controls and the oven and some plates have thermostats ensuring
that the temperature of each stays at the chosen level.

The controls may be sited on the front of the cooker or high
out of reach of children on the splash back. These are not
always sufficiently clearly marked so that you can immediately
see which switch works each part of the stove. On some stoves
with automatic timers the arrangements for switching from manual to automatic and for setting the cooking times are unneces-
sarily complicated. An electric cooker does not give as instant a
response to control as a gas cooker but in most cases this

problem lessens as you become accustomed to the cooker. It
used to be thought that the gas cooker was a quicker method of
cooking than electricity but in actual fact there is little to
choose between the two in the time taken for the initial heating
of a pan.

The Hob
The hob is usually fitted with three or four flameless boiling
rings. Any spillage on the rings themselves is quickly burnt away
and can be easily removed. The surrounding enamel needs only
to be wiped over occasionally with a damp cloth. There are two
types of rings, radiant rings and disc rings. Most cookers now
have radiant rings which are spiral tubes containing the element
which is sealed into the hob surface. Disc rings can be installed
separately into working surfaces and are often incorporated into
split level cooker schemes. The rings are available in several
sizes. There is also a dual ring which has a switch to turn on
either the centre part or the whole ring. Most stoves have at
least one burner with a thermostatic device. This has a central
sensing head the flat top of which is sprung so that it maintains
contact with a pan resting on it. The head transmits the heat
from the base of the pan to a thermostat which controls the
current. The contents of the pan are maintained at the temperature represented by the thermostat setting. The device is
mounted in the centre of the ring touching the underside of the
pan. It measures the temperature of the pan and keeps this at
the chosen setting. In this way milk does not overheat and boil
over or fat overflow or burn. Many cookers have built-in hob
lights. These may not be very powerful in themselves but may
be useful in supplementing the normal kitchen lighting. A recent
innovation is a glass ceramic topped hob. The hob is one complete sheet of scratch and stain resistant glass ceramic. It is very
easy to clean and the edges are sealed to prevent spillage seeping
inside.

The Grill
Most grills are now almost the full width of the cooker. In some
cookers it is possible for half the grill to be used on its own,
thus saving fuel when a small amount of food is to be grilled.
Most cookers have two or three grill pan runners so that you can

adjust the distance between the heat and the food. An increasing number of high level grills have rotating motor driven spits incorporated in them. In some cases the eye level grill section is fitted with a door and controls which enable you to use it as a second oven or as a plate warming compartment.

The Oven

The oven is a double walled steel box, the gap between the inner and outer walls being insulated with glass fibre and foil. There is just one small vent for the escape of steam. There is very little air movement so there is very little change of temperature inside the oven. Most double width ovens have a rotisserie spit and these may be supplied as an optional extra with the ordinary oven. A few have a roastmeter which is an adjustable thermo-meter inserted into the joint of meat and set at the required level. When the meat is cooked a buzzer sounds.

The oven is economical in the use of space as dishes and tins can be put within 1 cm of the walls. The elements are usually mounted behind the side walls of the oven. Some have elements below the floor. Electric cookers have accurate temperature controls from 110°-250°C. An indicator light, which goes on when the oven is switched on, goes out when it reaches the selected temperature. Many ovens have an automatic cooking timer.

Fan Assisted Ovens

Several of the latest models on the domestic market have fan assisted ovens. Until now these have only been available in large catering cookers. Instead of using two elements, one behind each side wall there is only one element placed behind the back panel of the oven. This element has a circular fin-like element surrounding a small fan. The fan and the element work to-gether. Neither can be switched on separately although the fan will continue to work to circulate heat when the element has been switched off by the thermostat. The hot air is blown around the oven. This is faster than depending on the convec-tion of heat so the oven heats up more quickly and stays at the required temperature while using less electricity. Cooking time is shorter, the food browns evenly on each shelf and there is less shrinkage in the case of cooked meats.

The Thermostat

The thermostat used on many electrical appliances consists of a bimetal strip which bends when heated. As it bends it opens the contact and disconnects the current. When it cools down it straightens out to make contact again and so turns on the electric current. The control switch determines just how much the strip must bend before the current is disconnnected.

Warming Compartment

This may be part of the grill section or may be incorporated into the base of the cooker in the form of a drawer. The wider cookers may have a small warming oven. The warming compartment may be warmed indirectly by the oven or have its own heating system.

Gas Cookers

Gas cooking is the most flexible. The visible flame can be turned up or lowered instantly. The modern cooker is designed to be easily controlled and cleaned. Gas cookers have the reputation for being difficult to clean. This is partially because the

gas burner must have a pan support with projections sited in such a way that the gas can burn in free air. This usually means that the pan supports are rather intricate and difficult to clean. In addition to this there is the fact that the gas in burning gives off water vapour. There is bound to be a certain amount of condensation and any dirt present is more likely to adhere to a wet surface than a dry one.

The Hotplate or Hob

This consists of the burners, the hotplate pressing and the pan supports. The design of this is governed by the need for gas to burn in free air for the maximum amount of heat to be transmitted to the pan and its contents. All burners are aerated and have fixed injectors. Burners may be open or solid rings or may be bar-shaped. There are differences in the perforations in the burners to allow for flames of different sizes. Some burners produce a small number of large flames while others produce many overlapping small flames. All hot plate burners have automatic ignition on the hotplate. The most usual system is one incorporating permanent pilots and flash tubes to the burners. Turning the gas tap causes the appropriate burner to light. Gas is a very flexible form of heating and this flexibility is improved by the use of thermostatically controlled burners similar to those on the electric stove.

The Grill

This is designed to give even heating over the whole cooking area. The frets are lightweight so that they heat up quickly. The grill cooks by infra red heat. The grill frets have covers which help to conserve the heat by reflecting back the infra red rays. Some grills diffuse the gas through metal gauze, this gives the same heat distribution to the food but is less intense.

Eye level grills are popular. These are often combined with an electrically driven spit rotisserie which may be adapted for cooking kebabs.

The Oven

Like the electric oven this is a double walled, insulated box. Air is drawn in, heated by the burners and circulated around the food placed on the oven shelves. Hot air rises so the top of the oven is usually a little hotter than the thermostat setting and the lower part a little cooler.

Bottle Gas Cookers

These look exactly like the ordinary gas stove but are run on butane gas. This gas is sold in cylinders for homes where there is no direct gas supply. It is usual to have two cylinders placed outside the house and connected through into the house. The gas regulator on the cylinders tends to freeze in very cold weather so it is sensible to protect the cylinders with lagging and a cover of some sort. It should not be difficult for an amateur carpenter to build a small cupboard around them. As soon as one cylinder is empty the second cylinder switches on without any variation in the pressure. The supplier will call at regular intervals. He can see from an indicator if one cylinder is empty and will replace it whether you are at home or not. The running cost of this type of fuel compares favourably with other fuels. Cooking by bottled gas is similar to cooking by ordinary gas. Butane gas produces a high proportion of water vapour so adequate ventilation is needed.

Solid Fuel Cookers

In the past solid fuel cookers were often wasteful of fuel and inefficient. They were also difficult to control. During recent years they have been greatly improved. Beyond refuelling twice a day they need very little attention and they never need to go out. All solid fuel stoves can be bought with a back boiler which should give ample hot water for the average household.

Heat Storage Cookers

The initial cost of a heat storage cooker and its installation is more than that of the average gas or electric cooker but if it is properly used it is economical to run. It is especially suitable for a household where a lot of cooking is done. A small continuously burning fire heats a thick metal casing. The heat is taken from this through conduction plates to the oven and the hot plates.

There are usually two very large hot plates. One is used for fast boiling and the other for simmering. Most cookers have two ovens, one for roasting or baking, and the other for slow cooking and plate warming. A thermostat is fitted. This controls the rate of burning of the fire and the heat of the ovens and hot plate. This is easy to set and easy to see. The cookers are so well insulated that there is very little heat loss and the kitchen does not get overheated. When they are not in use the hot plates are covered with heavily insulated lids. Heavy ground-base cooking utensils which make even contact with the hot plates should be used.

Most solid storage cookers are designed to use smokeless fuel only and in this case only very occasional chimney sweeping will be needed. Fuel consumption is low. Stoking, riddling and removal of ashes are easily carried out.

The cookers are covered in vitreous enamel in a number of attractive colours. They are easy to clean and very hard wearing.

Cleaning the Cooker
Most modern cookers are designed to be easy to clean. It has been said that if everyone, who after considering a certain model and rejecting it because of cleaning problems, wrote to the maker saying they had done so, many designs would soon be improved.

Follow the manufacturer's instruction for dismantling and cleaning. Make sure the gas or electric power is turned off. If you are using a proprietary oven cleanser follow the maker's instructions. Wear gloves. Protect your clothing and the area surrounding the cooker. Do not use a caustic cleanser on any aluminium parts of the cooker. Enzyme detergents are useful for soaking clean small parts.

The Hob or Hot Plate
Wipe up spillage as soon as it occurs before it has a chance to harden on the surface. A wipe over with a damp cloth once a day should be enough to ensure that lengthy cleaning operations will seldom be needed. Some cooker hobs are designed to be partially dismantled. This enables you to take the parts to be

cleaned to the sink. Some electric hobs have removable boiling rings. These must never be immersed in water but simply wiped over with a damp cloth. They are unlikely to get very dirty as they burn themselves clean. They are removed because this simplifies the cleaning of the rest of the hob.

Spillage burnt onto the surface of the hob can be removed with a soap-impregnated steel wool pad. If necessary a fine scouring powder may also be used. In extreme cases special oven cleaning preparations may be used. Follow the makers instructions. Take care to remove all traces of the preparation by rinsing the surface several times with clear water.

The Grill
The grill itself usually burns off most things deposited on it. Grill frets on a gas cooker may need an occasional rub with a wire or stiff nylon brush. High level grills will need to be wiped over regularly to remove grease deposited on them in the steam from the food being cooked on the hot plate below. Grills fitted between the hot plate and the spillage tray do get dirtied by particles falling through from the hot plate. The heat rising from such grills can cause burning of spillage onto the hot plate. Regular wiping down is necessary. Parts of the grill and the spillage tray may be removable. The grill pan should be treated as an ordinary cooking utensil and cleaned each time after use.

The Oven
Many ovens now being produced have PTFE non stick linings so that cleaning them is merely a matter of wiping down with a damp cloth. There are ovens which clean themselves automatically. The Pyrolitic system uses a thermostat with a very high temperature setting. At this heat all the encrusted grease and other food particles are burnt off. At the end of two hours this is a fine ash and the oven is clean. Should you purchase one of these ovens it is important to ensure that there is an effective locking device which prevents anyone opening the oven door while the temperature is high. In the continuous clean system the oven finish reacts to oxygen and destroys the splashes of grease as they are made.

Other less expensive ovens are designed so that cleaning is made as simple as possible with hinged or removable top and sides or removable linings. Drop down doors may be removable making it easier to reach the back of the oven. Try to avoid getting the oven dirty by using meat tins just large enough to contain the joint. This prevents fat being exposed to the heat and over-heated. Cover food being cooked. When cleaning is necessary use the same materials as for the hot plate. If you leave a saucer-ful of ammonia in the oven overnight you will find it easier to remove the grease. If you then wipe off the worst of the grease with a wad of newspaper the real cleaning will be easier.

Pressure Cookers
Most people think that the pressure cooker is a recent invention but it was actually invented in 1679 by a Frenchman, Denys Papin. John Evelyn records the use of a pressure cooker being used at a dinner given by the Royal Society in 1682. While the modern cooker is more accurate and of a better design than these early models the basic principle remains the same, yet it is undoubtedly of more use nowadays than it was when it was invented, when servants were plentiful.

When food is cooked in liquid or steam in an ordinary pan under normal atmospheric pressure the temperature of the food cannot be raised above the boiling point of the liquid. This is 100°C for water and slightly higher for liquids containing sugar, salt and other dissolved solids. No matter how much heat is applied to the pan the food cannot cook more quickly. If you could expel the air from the saucepan and seal in the steam, pressure would be created in the pan. As the pressure increased there would be a rise in temperature. This speeds up the cooking saving fuel and nutritive value and colour.

The pressure cooker is a pan designed to carry out these functions. Domestic pressure cookers may be either casserole or saucepan models and are available in a range of sizes from 3 to 18 litres. It is sensible to choose one slightly larger than that needed for daily use. It is just as economical in fuel and time to cook a small amount of food in a large cooker as in a small one.

The saucepan type is of conventional shape with a long handle on both cover and base and a small side handle to facilitate lifting. It may have a flat or domed cover depending on the size of the cooker. The casserole type has a small handle on either side and a flat cover.

In both types the cover of the cooker is secured in such a way as to make it impossible for it to lift as the pressure inside the pan builds up.

All cookers have safety devices which operate should the pressure rise above the maximum for which the cooker has been designed. This is usually in the form of a rubber plug which melts at 140°C. This may happen if the pan boils dry or if the automatic air vent becomes blocked by grease, food or dirt. Should this happen you should check the air vent and clean it if necessary and ensure that there is sufficient liquid in the cooker before replacing the plug.

A few cookers are fitted with pressure gauges. The pressure can be controlled in the majority of cookers and this control usually incorporates a working device such as a whistle which operates when the desired pressure has been used. Some cookers are supplied with dividers or wire racks so that several different foods can be cooked at the same time. There are models available for gas and electric cookers. Remember to choose a cooker with a ground base if you cook on solid hot plates on an electric or solid fuel cooker.

Before cooking in a pressure cooker you should carefully study the manufacturer's instruction booklet. Make sure you are familiar with each part of the cooker. The directions for sealing the cooker and controlling the pressure should be practised until they are mastered.

Keep the manufacturer's instructions near at hand when you start using the cooker, until you are confident that you can control the cooker without referring to them.

Using a Pressure Cooker
1 The cooker should never be filled too full. As a rule it should be half filled for liquid and semi-liquid food and two thirds filled for solid food.
2 The lid should be put into position and the cooker put over a high heat. When it starts to steam the pressure control device should be adjusted as directed in the manufacturer's instructions.
3 The contents of the cooker should be brought up to the required pressure. The heat should then be reduced. Cooking time should be calculated from this moment.

4 The cooking times given in charts and recipes should be followed but there are bound to be slight variations due to weight, thickness and texture of food and to the gas pressure or electricity loading. If in doubt it is better to cook for a shorter time than that suggested to avoid over cooking. If necessary you can always bring back the pressure and cook the food a little longer.

5 *Never* attempt to open the pan before the pressure has dropped to normal as force is exerting against the pan and the lid. The handles should slide apart easily or the lid unlock without difficulty. The pressure can be reduced quickly by holding the pan under cold water for 10 to 15 seconds. Lift the weight or lever of the control device slightly. If there is no hissing sound you can raise it fully and then open the pan. For the slow method take the cooker off the hob and leave it to cool down for about 10 minutes until the weight or lever can be raised without any hissing being heard.

Care of the Cooker

Wash the cooker very carefully after use. Check and wash the vent. Make sure the gasket or sealing ring is free of grease and food particles. Dry the cooker thoroughly. Do not store it with the lid closed as it will soon become musty.

3 Large Appliances

Refrigerators

After the cooker, the refrigerator is probably the next most important piece of equipment in the kitchen. It is designed to keep food fresh and clean.

Refrigerators are ideal for the storage of food because:

1 The temperature inside the refrigerator is maintained irrespective of the changes of temperature outside. The temperature of the kitchen in winter is often higher than during the summer.

2 The temperature of the inside of the refrigerator is low enough to slow down the activity of bacteria.

3 The food compartment is enclosed. Food cannot be contaminated by dust and insects.

4 A refrigerator cuts down food wastage. Food does not deteriorate quickly. Surplus food can be saved and used later.

5 Shopping is simplified as perishable foods do not have to be purchased at frequent intervals.

6 Dishes can be prepared in advance and stored. This simplifies meal planning and entertaining.

7 Many foods taste better for being chilled.

Cooling is brought about by the evaporation of a liquid (the refrigerant) which flows through the tubes forming the evaporator. As it takes up the heat from the inside of the refrigerator the refrigerant vaporises and is turned back into a liquid to start the cycle all over again.

The Cabinet

This is composed of an outer shell and a lining. The lining nowadays is usually plastic although metal finish with enamel or special paint is equally suitable. The outer shell is usually painted metal although there are some finished with plastic laminates. The space between the outer shell and lining is filled with an insulating material which is a non-conductor of heat such as glass wool or plastic foam. The door is constructed in a similar way. A plastic or rubber gasket in which a magnet is fitted seals the door. This ensures a perfect seal when the door is closed. No air can pass through this seal.

A dial inside the refrigerator controls the thermostat which keeps the temperature constant at the desired level. The manufacturer's handbook should explain the settings of each model. Once set the thermostat should only need adjusting in very hot weather.

The least cool part of the refrigerator is the interior of the door which is usually fitted with racks for the storage of milk, butter, eggs, etc. The coldest section is the compartment formed by the refrigerant tubes, the evaporator at the top of the refrigerator. In most refrigerators this section, the frozen food compartment, is marked with one, two, or three stars to indicate the temperature and the length of time frozen food can be stored in the evaporator. Commercially frozen foods will have these star marks on the wrappings.

One star*   indicates that the temperature in the frozen food compartment of this model is approximately -6°C and frozen food can be stored for up to 1 week.

Two stars** Temperature approximately -12°C Storage time up to 4 weeks.

Three stars   Temperature approximately -18°C Storage time up
***   to 3 months.

Compartments which are not star marked may only be suitable for making ice cubes. They usually operate at above -6°C. Frozen foods should not be stored for more than one or two days.

Most cabinets are equipped with shelves and special containers for vegetables, salads, raw meat and fish. Trays for making ice cubes can be fitted into the evaporator section.

The size of the refrigerator will depend on the size of the family and on the space available in the kitchen. Running costs are low enough not to influence the choice of the model. It is sensible to choose the largest model you can afford that will fit into your kitchen. It has been shown that once a refrigerator has been bought the maximum use is always made of it. It is impractical to buy one less than 0.1 cubic metres in size though smaller models may be useful in caravans or flatlets. There are many shapes to choose from. You can have low models at table height to provide extra working surfaces, tall slim models which take up little floor space and others designed to be built into kitchen units. A small refrigerator can be fixed to a wall. Doors can be hinged to open from the left or right handside.

Using the Refrigerator

1 Manufacturers' instructions should be followed strictly.
2 Always cool food to room temperature before placing it in the refrigerator. This reduces the running costs and cuts down the amount of ice forming on the evaporator.

3 Food is best covered to prevent it drying out or crossing flavours with other foods. Use plastic boxes with lids, screw top jars, polythene bags, foil or plastic wrappings.
4 Food should only be stored for the recommended time.

Storing of Food in the Refrigerator

Food is placed according to the storage temperature it requires. The frozen food compartment is the coolest part. The temperature rises slightly towards the lower sections of the cabinet. The food should be arranged in the following order if directions are not given with the refrigerator.

Frozen food compartment—Ice cube trays, storage of frozen food and ice cream
1st and 2nd shelves—Uncooked meats, poultry, offal, sausages, fish
3rd shelf—Cooked meat, pies, gravy, cheese
4th shelf—Bacon, milk dishes, cold sweets
Bottom drawer—Salad, green vegetables, fruit
Door racks—Butter, eggs and milk

Avoid storing strong smelling fruits such as melons, strawberries and pineapples. If you wish to chill them wrap them well and leave in the refrigerator for a short time only. Bananas should not be stored as they will turn black.

Defrosting the Refrigerator

Moisture drawn from the air in the cabinet freezes on the surface of the evaporator. Once it has collected to the thickness of about a centimetre it needs to be removed otherwise the refrigerator will work less efficiently. While many refrigerators must be defrosted manually many are now defrosted semi or fully automatically. For *semi-automatic defrosting* a special defrost button must be pressed. This stops the refrigeration system and the ice melts. When the defrosting is over the refrigerator cycle starts up again. Some models have a rapid defrosting device which introduces heat into the evaporator. Follow the manufacturer's instructions regarding the removal of food. Fully automatic defrosting needs no attention. As the name suggests it takes place automatically at frequent intervals. There is no build-up of ice and therefore no need to remove the food.

Manual Defrosting

1 Turn control dial to 'off' or 'defrost'.
2 Remove all the food from the refrigerator. Wrap frozen food in thick layers of newspaper and put it in a cool place.
3 Scrape off ice with a brush or a wooden spatula. Collect as much ice as possible before it thaws and dispose of it into the sink.
4 A bowl of warm water in the refrigerator will speed up the defrosting process. The melting ice will collect as water in the drip tray, which can be removed and emptied.
5 Wipe out the refrigerator.
6 Reset the controls and replace the food.

Cleaning

This is normally done each time the refrigerator is defrosted; manually and at regular intervals if the defrosting is automatic.

Freezers

Food must be frozen at a temperature below -2°C. At these temperatures enzyme action is slowed down so that the food stays in good condition for a long period.

The owner of a home freezer can purchase fruit and vegetable in bulk when they are in season and at their best and at the lowest price. They can be stored to be used later when they would normally not be available or would be very expensive. Surplus fruit and vegetables from the garden can be stored for future use. Meat and poultry and ready frozen foods can be bought in bulk at discount prices. Many major companies and independently run frozen food depots supply foods at wholesale prices. Most offer free delivery services. A good source of addresses is the quarterly magazine called *Freeze*.

Shopping time can be cut to the minimum as the housewife will not need to make frequent journeys to replenish perishable food stocks. The housewife can cut down the time spent in the preparation of food by preparing batches of dishes and freezing those she does not need immediately for future use. Entertaining can be more enjoyable if there is no need for last minute shopping and food preparation. It is possible to have a variety of appetising meals available at all times.

Anyone contemplating buying a freezer should buy or borrow a comprehensive book on the subject in order to learn how to make the very best use of the appliance. There are many available. Make sure you know the difference between a conservator and a freezer. A conservator maintains a temperature of -18°C but is only suitable for storing food which is already frozen. A freezer on the other hand will go down to -21°C so that you can freeze your own produce.

Size of Freezer
It is usual to allow about ¼ cubic metre of space for each person. It is sensible to buy a size larger than you think you need. Most people find that, once they have learned to use the freezer efficiently, they use up all the available space and would like more.

One tenth of the freezer's capacity can be used for freezing food each day. The larger the freezer the less the cost per cubic capacity. Very large freezers are expensive and it would be stupid to buy space you will not use. Empty space uses more electricity to keep cold than does frozen food. You will get more real value from the freezer if there is a constant turnover of the contents rather than using it for very long term storage. You should be able to get advice on the size most suitable for your needs from the Electricity Board or from the dealer. If possible discuss the matter with someone who already owns a freezer. A large freezer is heavy and even heavier when filled with food. Make sure the floor is strong enough to take this weight.

Rules for Freezing
1 Read the instruction book supplied with the freezer. This may give instructions in the use of the specific cabinet.
2 Freeze only food in perfect condition as soon as possible after gathering and preparing.
3 Wrap in moisture and vapour proof materials.
4 Never put hot foods into the freezer. Cool them quickly first.
5 Set the controls at the coldest setting several hours before freezing food. Follow instructions for freezing in book provided or in a freezer cook-book.
6 Do not store food for longer than the recommended time.
7 Thaw and use as recommended.

Foods which freeze successfully include most vegetables and fruits, poultry, meat, raw pastry, bread and other yeast products, cakes and puddings.

Foods which do not freeze successfully include salad vegetables with a high water content, fruits such as bananas, melons and pears, milk, eggs in shells, mayonnaise, bacon and onions.

Packaging Materials
It is important to have a selection of packaging materials always at hand. If food is not packed properly loss of moisture by dehydration can occur. Packaging should ensure that there is no interchange of flavours and odours.

The following materials will be useful.
1 Polythene bags and sheets of polythene. (150-200 gauge)
2 Waxed cartons (can be saved from other commodities such as cream and yoghourt)
3 Foil and foil dishes and plates
4 Special freezer paper
5 Plastic boxes
6 Specially designed glass containers (Pyroceram). Do not use ordinary glass as it is not designed for cold storage, it cannot stand the low temperature.

Packaging can be re-used provided it is handled carefully and washed and dried thoroughly. Each packet should be clearly marked with the date, contents, and weight. They should be carefully sealed using special freezer tape or covered wire fasteners.

A record book should be kept to ensure that foods are used in rotation. Records should be kept of all foods put into the freezer and those taken out so that you have an up-to-date account of stocks.

Most of the other utensils necessary for preparing food for freezing are those to be found in the average kitchen.

Defrosting
Many of the modern freezers defrost themselves automatically but most models will need defrosting every 9 to 12 months depending on the usage of the cabinet. Should a thick layer of frost accumulate at a time when defrosting is inconvenient the excess frost can be brushed off and collected. Try to arrange to defrost the freezer when food stocks are low.
1 Wrap up food packs in thick layers of newspaper. Put them in a cool place such as the refrigerator, or in an unheated room or shed.
2 Turn off the electricity.
3 Scrape off the frost with a wooden spatula or a brush and remove this while it is still frozen.
4 Wipe out the cabinet using warm water. If it is necessary to remove grease or smells add a teaspoon of bicarbonate of soda to each litre of water. For strong smells use two table-

spoons of vinegar to each litre of water and rinse with clear water.

5 Turn on the electricity. Allow the temperature of the cabinet to fall before replacing the food.

Emergency Measures

Most freezers are very reliable but power cuts and mechanical breakdowns could happen and it is as well to be prepared for them even if they never occur. Everyone who purchases a freezer should get user instructions which should be followed in an emergency. Most freezers will keep food in good condition for up to 24 hours if the door is not opened. The more food in the cabinet the longer will the temperature remain down should the power be cut. Buyers should check that a 24 hour repair service is available. If the freezer cannot be repaired quickly or a replacement provided make sure that the service organisation can transfer the food to a cold store.

Should all the normal repair services fail or the power cut last longer than 24 hours, you may be able to store the food at a frozen food locker centre (if they still have power themselves) or you may be able to get a supply of dry ice, (see Yellow Pages Telephone Directory for local supplier). Wear gloves when handling this. You can insure against power failure or mechanical breakdown. Premiums vary between £2.25 and £5.25 per £100 worth of food but could be less if your insurance company will extend your household comprehensive policy.

A Guide to Temperatures

Centigrade	Fahrenheit	
4° to 7°	40° to 47°	Average temperature inside domestic refrigerator
0°	32°	Freezing point of water
−6°	21°	Temperature in frozen food compartment in 1 star refrigerator
−12°	10°	Temperature in frozen food compartment in 2 star refrigerator

−18°	0°	Temperature in frozen food compartment in 3 star refrigerator
−18°	0°	Conservator storage temperature
−21°	−5°	Temperature for freezing fresh products
−34°	−30°	Temperature at which food is frozen commercially

Dishwashing Machines

The average housewife spends over 500 hours per year washing up by hand. It is not surprising that most owners of dishwashing machines are happy with their investment. For some reason many people accept the fact that a washing machine is essential while regarding a dishwasher as a luxury. Not only does a dishwasher save time and labour, it also does the job of dish washing much more efficiently than it is possible to do by hand. It is possible to use stronger detergents and hotter water than hands can bear. Although some of the washing cycles do seem to take a long time the machine does not have to be supervised so the homemaker is free to leave the machine once she has loaded it and set the controls. Dishwashing does not need to be done after every meal, only when the machine is full. Dirty dishes can be neatly stacked in the machine, out of sight. A dishwasher is an expensive piece of equipment so it is sensible to learn as much as possible about the various models in order to find the one most suitable for the needs of the household. Study all the manufacturers brochures or better still their instruction books. Choice will be limited by cost which can vary from about £70 to £350.

Types of Dishwashers

1 *Freestanding*. Cabinet complete with sides and top which does not need to be built on to working units. It may be permanently connected to water and electricity supplies.
2 *A portable* dishwasher is not permanently connected to water or electricity supplies. It is mounted on heavy castors or wheels and is light enough to be moved around the kitchen. These are useful for people who rent their homes for whom it would be impractical to 'build-in'.

3 Dishwashers designed so that with slight modifications they can be changed readily into a *freestanding, table, wall-mounted* or *under-counter* model.

4 *Under-counter* types are permanently connected to the water and electricity supplies. They may be built in to match other kitchen units.

5 *Automatic* dishwashers can be set to a required washing cycle and need no further attention by the user. Some machines have only one washing programme but others give a choice of several.

6 *Front loading* or *top loading.* The choice depends on personal preference. The majority of machines are front loaded to leave room above as a working surface.

Size and Shape

Dishwashers vary in shape and size but it is possible to purchase
a model to suit nearly every home. As a general guide:

Width ranges from 52-62 cms
Depth ranges from 44-62 cms
Height ranges from 50-86 cms

Front opening models will need at least 55 cms of clear space in
front of them.

Space will be needed at the back of the machine for the pipes.

Capacity is usually measured by the number of place settings a
machine will hold and wash at once. The number varies between
4 and 14 place settings.

A place setting consists of:

1 soup plate, 1 dinner plate, 1 flat dessert plate, 1 saucer, 1 cup,
1 glass, 1 knife, 1 fork, 1 teaspoon, 1 tablespoon, 1 dessert-
spoon plus a few additional serving pieces and utensils.

Plumbing

Machines permanently connected to the cold or hot water
system are more convenient to use than those fitted by a
hose attached to a tap. The machine may be plumbed to the hot
or cold system. The water will be heated in the machine to the
required temperature. Connecting to the hot water system will
cut down the time taken to complete the cycle. Cold water connection will not make demands on the domestic hot water
supply and the housewife can take advantage of rinse and hold
programmes. Most dishwashers use far less hot water for a single
load than when used for washing and rinsing the dishes by hand.

Using the Machine

1 Most household crockery and cutlery is suitable for machine
washing. These include those made of stainless steel, silver
plate so long as it is unworn, and heat resistant plastics. The
items which should not be machine washed are painted glass
or china, old silver plate, lead crystal glasswear, and articles
with wood bone or plastic handles especially those attached
by glue type fixatives.

2 The dishwasher is not a waste disposal unit. Leavings of food,
bones, tea leaves and ashtray contents should be removed

before loading the dishes into the machine. Cooking utensils can be machine washed but if food is baked on hard it would be as well to soak it first to loosen the food.

3 Care must be taken not to overload the machine as this will prevent the water circulating freely. Most manufacturers give clear instructions on loading these which should be followed carefully. Cups and glass should be placed open end down so that water cannot form puddles inside. Bowls and plates on lower racks should not be allowed to impede water reaching the upper rack.

4 Ordinary household detergents are not suitable for machines. Use one of the detergents recommended by the manufacturer and preferably the one approved by the British Ceramics Research Association. Detergents contain chemicals for water softening, removing grease and protein based stains, germicides and cleaning agents. In addition they contain tarnish inhibitors to protect silverwear and form suppressants to prevent too many suds forming. A chemical may be added to the final rinse to reduce water tension. This helps to prevent water spotting and streaking.

5 Dishes are washed by water being forced around the dishes under pressure. The main ways of circulating this water is by using an impellor or a spray. The impellor method involves a revolving blade built into the base of the machine. This blade causes the water to be tumbled outward, upward and into a spiral. The other method has a water driven turbine type water spray. This is more efficient mechanically and is quieter in use than the impellor type.

6 The washing cycle takes from 15-90 minutes depending on the machine and on the chosen programme. The dishes will be washed, rinsed and dried and can be left in the machine until you have time to store them away or until the next meal.

Most machines have a filter for food particles. This should be emptied and cleaned each time the machine is used.

Waste Disposal Unit
Waste disposal units are becoming increasingly popular with people living in both old and new homes. Refuse disposal is a

problem causing concern for many local authorities. The organic waste from the kitchen is attractive to flies and an ideal breeding ground for harmful organisms. Should you live in a house with a garden this waste can be carefully composted to make fertiliser for your garden. You can easily wrap it up in paper and put it straight into a dustbin in the garden away from the kitchen. If you live in a block of flats your problem is not so easily solved. The rubbish has to be taken down to the dustbin every day if it is not to become a smelly health hazard.

A waste disposer is an electrically powered grinding machine fitted to the waste pipe under the kitchen sink. The machine grinds the waste to a pulp fine enough to be washed down the waste pipe. Any food waste, including bones, fruit and vegetable skins, nutshells, egg shells, tea leaves can be disposed of by the machine. It can also deal with cigarette ends, matches, glass, china and soft paper. It cannot cope with string, cloth, cans, rubber or plastic.

The waste disposer can be fitted to the ordinary kitchen sink provided it has an outlet of 9 cms in diameter. Stainless steel and plastic sinks with a smaller outlet can sometimes be converted by enlarging the outlet. If the kitchen is a large one dealing with the needs of many people, and perhaps fitted with a dishwasher, it might be worth while having a special disposer sink. This is a tiny sink with a water supply intended just for waste disposal. Its use leaves the main sink free for other cleaning activities. Apart from the sink itself the waste pipe must be large enough to carry the pulverised waste and set at a steep enough angle to ensure that the waste matter will not block the pipe. There must be an electric point near the sink. Given these factors installation should not be unduly expensive.

Choosing a Waste Disposer
There are two main types of disposal units. The batch-type holds a certain amount of waste material at one time and this must be pulverised before more is added. It will only work with the guard lid fitted. The machine automatically stops if the lid is removed. It is much safer in use than the continuous feed type. This will pulverise and dispose of rubbish continuously. Young children could not only put scraps but also their hands into the

mouth of the machine easily touching its cutting blades. Most machines have a cutlery guard and an automatic cut out device. Some have a reversing switch which can be used to reverse the action of the blade. If this is used regularly the wear on both sides of the cutting blades can be equalised. The reversing switch can also be used to free any waste which may be clogging the works. In the past the breakdown of a disposer unit meant that the sink was put out of use until repairs could be carried out. A model now on the market has a device which enables the homemaker to continue to use the sink. The noise level varies with different machines. Some have built-in acoustic hoods.

Using the Waste Disposer

1 It is important to read the manufacturer's instructions and to follow them carefully.
2 Do not try to dispose of anything other than the things recommended by the manufacturer. Make sure you do not throw out teaspoons, teapot lids or salt cellars by mistake.
3 Do not allow young children to use the machine. Have the switch installed high up out of their reach. Switch off the machine if you leave the sink even for a short time if there are children in the house.

4 Most detergents and bleaches used for laundry purposes are harmless to the machine if used as a weak solution. Avoid strong solutions, or chemical drain cleaners as these could damage the machinery. Occasional use of mild disinfectants would probably do no harm but they are not necessary as everything is washed away before it has a chance to dirty the machine. The waste disposer is self-cleaning provided the water is allowed to run freely for a while after the grinding chamber has been emptied of waste.

5 Should the machine jam the electric power should be switched off immediately. Do not attempt to free blockage inside the machine by hand. All manufacturers warn against this. Release keys and dejamming devices are often supplied for minor jams. If this does not work you should send for the maintenance engineer. Do not try to open the machine to release the blockage. There is an after sales service for all the machines on the market at present.

6 The waste disposer is very inexpensive to run and if used sensibly should last for up to 12 years in the average home.

4 Electrical Appliances

Well chosen electrical appliances can be an asset to any house although they will be of little value and will not save labour unless suitable for the job you want them to do. You should be able to get up-to-date information at the Electricity Board showrooms about all the different makes and models available in this country. You can check on the efficiency or safety of any model at the local Consumers Advice Centre or from the British Electrical Approvals Board. Your local Electricity Board will supply the address.

Make sure your electricity supply and power points are suitable for the loading rate of the appliance. Never use them in a lamp or lighting point. Before you purchase an appliance inquire about servicing facilities and availability of spare parts.

Details of cookers, deep freezers, refrigerator and water heaters are given in other chapters. Here we are concerned with smaller portable appliances.

Food Mixers and Blenders
A food mixer can save a great deal of time and labour in the preparation of meals provided you choose one suitable for the work you intend it to do and of the right size to deal with the quantities of food normally used by the family. It is sensible to

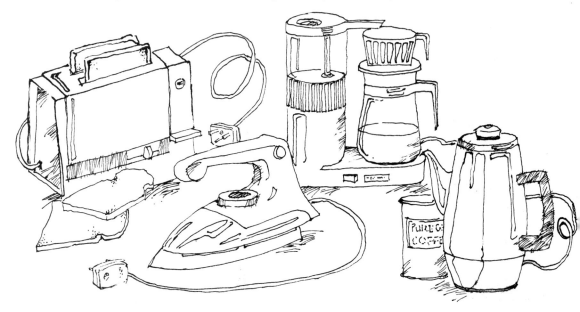

study the many different machines on the market before
making a choice. The final choice may lie anywhere between a
large food preparation machine and a small hand mixer. Before
making a decision there are a number of things you should do.

1 Look at as many different types and makes as possible so
   that you know what is available at the price you can afford.
2 Try to have a demonstration of any mixer which particularly
   interests you. If possible try using the mixer yourself.
3 Check for safety. Ideally the mixer should carry the approval
   of the British Electrical Approvals Board (BEAB).
4 Find out a The number of speeds for mixing.
           b What attachments are included in the cost and
              those which are optional extras.
           c For how long the machine can run continuously.
           d The quantity of food it will process.
           e The amount of noise it makes.
           f The ease of cleaning the machine after use.
5 Enquire about spare parts and servicing arrangements. Make
   sure spare parts are immediately available, that there is a
   servicing centre in your district and that repairs can be carried
   out within a reasonable time. This is an especially important
   precaution to take when buying an imported machine.
6 Study the manufacturers instruction book and recipe book.
   The recipe book should give you some idea about the amount
   of work the machine can do. If the instruction book does not
   give you sufficiently clear instructions about using the

machine and on fixing and using attachments ask the dealer for further information.

The Work of the Machine

The size and power of the machine will decide how much it can do but generally it can be expected to carry out the following operations:

Rubbing in fat to flour for pastry, scones, biscuits
Creaming fat and sugar
Beating cake mixes, eggs, potatoes
Whisking egg whites
Mixing batters and sauces
Whipping cream
Kneading yeast mixtures

Attachments

The motor of the mixer can be used to run a number of attachments. These may include blenders, juice extractors and separators, mincers, coffee grinders, potato peelers, shredders and slicers, bean slicers, pea huller, colander and sieves and can openers.

Attachments take up less storage space than separate gadgets such as individual blenders and mincers. They can be bought separately as the need arises and your budget can afford them.

Using a Food Mixer

1 The mixer should be kept available and ready for use when required.
2 Follow the manufacturers instructions.
3 Use the correct beater for the type of job.
4 Use the correct speed. Follow manufacturers instructions but as a general guide use low speeds for rubbing in mixtures, medium for creamed mixtures and high speed for whisking.
5 Do not overwork the machine. Do not use more than the recommended quantities of food. Never operate the motor for more than 5 minutes without a break as this might damage the motor.
6 Should the machine seem to be labouring reduce the quantity of food immediately.

7 If the mixture comes too far up the side of the bowl, stop the machine. Scrape the mixture from the sides back into the bottom of the machine using a plastic spatula. Start again at a lower speed.
8 Care must be taken not to overbeat mixtures. Until you are experienced in using the machine follow instructions carefully, watch constantly and stop the machine at intervals until the right consistency is reached.
9 Switch off and unplug before cleaning.
10 The bowl and beaters should be washed in hot soapy water and dried. The motor unit must never be immersed in water. Wipe over metal or plastic parts with a slightly damp cloth.
11 When not in use the mixer should be covered. Hand mixers should be hung in the wall rack usually supplied with them.

Blenders

Blenders are extremely versatile pieces of equipment. They vary in power, price and design though they are basically similar. They are generally used to complement the work of a food mixer but in some cases they are even more useful. Given the choice of a mixer or a blender it is likely that most good cooks would choose the latter. The type of work carried out depends on the power of the machine and the food to be processed but it can be used for practically every meal each day to help with food preparation.

The usual jobs that a blender will do include:
Blending sauces, soups, batters, baby foods, and mayonnaise
Pulping fruit and vegetables
Mincing cooked meat and fish
Shredding vegetables
Chopping fruit, vegetables, cheese, chocolate, mint, parsley
Puree or liquidizing fruit
Grinding nuts, coffee, sugar
Crumbling bread, cake, biscuits
Whipping drinks

Using the Blender
1 Keep the blender ready and available for use.
2 The blender should only be run for short periods to avoid overheating the motor. Allow the machine to cool down between each session.

3 Do not overload the blender. Follow manufacturers instructions as to the quantities to process. If there is a large quantity of food to be blended divide it into small amounts. As a general rule only half fill the goblet with liquids and do not switch on the motor before capping the goblet. If you forget to do this you are likely to spatter yourself and the kitchen with the contents of the goblet.

4 Wash the goblet immediately after use to prevent food particles drying on the sides. Half fill the goblet with hot water. Add a little detergent. Operate the blender for a few seconds. Empty the blender and rinse it well in clear warm water. Dry with a cloth or leave upside down to drain. Do not wash the goblet in a dishwasher as this could damage the seal between the blades and the goblet.

5 Switch off and unplug the blender before cleaning the motor unit. Never immerse the motor unit in water. Wipe it over with a slightly damp cloth.

Electric kettles

An electric kettle is very useful as it enables you to boil water anywhere in the house where there is a suitable electric point. If you cook by electricity it is less expensive to boil water in an electric kettle than in an ordinary kettle on the stove. A kettle with a high loading of 2000-3000 watts will bring water to the boil very rapidly while a kettle with a low loading of 1000 watts takes a little longer. These kettles should be used with a 13 or 15 amp plug. Kettle capacities vary from 1 to 3 litres.

The kettle should always be filled to the level suggested by the manufacturers to ensure that the heating element is submerged. It should be fitted with a safety cut out to prevent damage should the kettle boil dry. One type operates on a thermostatic principle, the electrical current being cut off when the kettle reaches a certain temperature and being turned on when the kettle cools. Another type has a device which forces out the plug from the kettle should it boil dry. The kettle must be reset by pushing in the ejector pin before the kettle can be used again.

Some models switch themselves off as soon as they reach boiling point so there is no risk of the room being filled with steam. Others have whistles which operate as soon as boiling point is reached.

Electric kettles are usually made of aluminium or of chrome on copper with a tinned interior. The latter is the more durable and therefore the more expensive. It is now possible to purchase a kettle with a body of plastic strong enough to withstand and contain boiling water but not conducting heat to the outside, the top is stainless steel and the handle is also made of plastic modified polyphenylene oxide (MPPO).

Electric Frying Pan or the Multipurpose Cooker
The name 'frying pan' is not a very good name for an appliance which apart from frying, can bake, boil, griddle, braise, stew and roast. There are few cooking jobs it cannot cope with. It is ideal for use in a small flat or bedsitting room where cooking facilities are limited. With a separate gas or electric hob the cook should be able to manage quite well without an oven or grill. In the conventional kitchen it is a most useful additional appliance.

They are very inexpensive to run as they use only about a fifth of the electricity as compared with an oven. The thermostat is controlled by a knob in the handle. There are several models available of various sizes with different types of lids and containers. One model, at present the most expensive, has a removable control socket. This simplifies cleaning as once this is removed the whole pan can be immersed in water.

Mini-Cookers
Not everyone has a large kitchen with space for a full size cooker or split level oven and hob. Many people live in single rooms or in very tiny flats where the 'kitchen' is a fitted cupboard or a set of shelves behind a screen. In many cases a full size cooker would be superfluous even if there was a space. For a person who has most of her meals away from home and merely needs a cooker for breakfast and cold snacks a large oven is wasteful in space and use of fuel. A single person living alone with few visitors does not need the same size oven as that needed by a family. If the accommodation is to be temporary, as it would probably be for a student or a young person

working away from home for a time, the cost of purchasing a mini-cooker could be less than even renting a family sized model.

Many of the electric mini-cookers can be used from a 13 or 15 amp power point so that there is no need for elaborate fitting or disconnecting. However it is important that the loading of each part of an electric cooker is known so that there is no danger of overloading the circuits. The total loading of the appliance, hob and oven must not exceed 3 kilowatts.

Gas mini-cookers can be run off bottled gas so that they do not have to be connected to the gas mains. This could be an advantage should the electrical power be insufficient or unreliable. It is possible to purchase an oven unit quite separately from the hob top and grill. The units can fit into a counter top, or be hung on a wall or used on a trolley.

It is important when purchasing mini-ovens not to purchase one that is too small to be practical. You are hardly likely to need to roast a large turkey in such an oven but it should be large enough to take a joint, a full sized chicken or a large cake. One large boiling plate is insufficient. There should be at least two otherwise it is likely to take so long to cook an ordinary meal that there may be the temptation to avoid cooking essential foods.

The cooker need not be discarded should you move into a home with a full sized kitchen. Many people find them invaluable for use when cooking for one or two members of the family or as an extra cooker when entertaining a number of guests. They can be used for keeping food and dishes warm or for cooking a single dish which needs a different temperature from the food in the main oven. Bottled gas cookers can be fitted into caravans or even be used when camping so long as you are travelling by car!

Toasters

Toast can be made under the grill but a toaster does the job automatically. No supervision is needed, there is less danger of toast being burnt and time and bread being wasted. Another toaster combines this function with that of a miniature grill. It has a side opening so that not only can it be used to toast bread but can also grill bacon, sausages, or mushrooms.

Other Electrical Appliances

New appliances or improvements incorporated into existing ones are constantly becoming available. Here are a few more which might prove useful:

1 An electric carving knife
2 An electric knife and scissors sharpener
3 A can opener
4 Plastic bag sealer—very useful if you prepare a lot of food for deep freezing
5 Coffee grinder
6 Jug immersion heaters for boiling very small amounts of liquid
7 Electric deep fat fryer
8 Coffee maker
9 Rotisserie grill
10 Waffle iron

5 Kitchen Utensils

One needs to spend a suprisingly large amount of money to purchase good quality kitchen utensils. If you are limited in the amount of money you can spend it is sensible to use this to purchase good quality, basic, essential tools rather than a wide variety of cheap goods. You can add to your basic tools later as and when money is available. By then you will have learned which extra pieces will be really useful to you. Every piece you acquire should be of definite use, be efficient, hardwearing and easily cared for.

Never buy any 'labour saving' gadget which is difficult to put together or to dismantle or clean. It will probably take more time and effort than it would take to do the work with a more conventional tool.

Make sure all kitchen utensils are suitably stored and readily available. clean them according to the manufacturers' instruction or according to the material from which they are made. Keep them sharpened and oiled where this is appropriate. Kitchen utensils should be checked regularly. Broken equipment which cannot be repaired and is of no further use should be discarded and not allowed to clutter up valuable storage space.

WIZZO BUTTER SPREADER

The utensils you will need depend on the size of the family and the amount and variety of cooking to be done. In this chapter various utensils will be placed in two lists—basic tools and those which are not essential. Descriptions will be given of most, but not all, of the items listed. Most of the utensils will be quite familiar to you but there may be a few you have never seen or even heard about before. You can probably add to the lists some gadget or utensil you have found to be especially useful in your kitchen at home or in school. You may know of others such as those used in kitchens overseas but seldom in this country which could usefully be added to the list.

Kitchen Knives etc.	
Basic	*Non essential*
Vegetable knife	Bread knife, potato peeler
Filleting knife	Freezer knife, meat saw
Cook's knife	Chopper or cleaver
Palette knife	Mandoline Hachoir
Steel or sharpener	Grapefruit knife Apple corer
	Stainless steel fruit knife

A set of good knives should last for a great number of years. It is well worth while spending as much as you can afford on the best quality knives. Choose the knives suitable for the jobs they are intended to do. They will then be easy and comfortable to use. The blade should be of a material which can take a fine edge. Traditionally this would be carbon steel which is the best metal for taking and keeping a fine edge. This material has one drawback in that it discolours so must be cleaned fairly frequently, because of this many people now choose stainless steel knives. If the stainless steel is of good quality with a high proportion of carbon and molybdenum it can be sharpened almost as finely as carbon steel.

Make sure the tang of the knife continues through almost the whole length of the handle. The handle should be riveted to the tang or glued with a good quality heat-resistant plastic adhesive. The handle may be of plain wood, plastic impregnated wood or plastic.

These are indispensable tools so they should be looked after
carefully. They should be kept clean, dry and well sharpened.
Learn to use a steel, this gives a finer edge than a sharpener. If
you use a sharpener follow the manufacturers instructions carefully as if you do not use this properly you are liable to sharpen
the knife with an uneven edge. The steel will not wear out the
knife as quickly as will the sharpener. Knives with hollow
ground blades or serrated fluted edges must be sent away to be
ground by a professional.

Store the knives carefully, out of reach of small children. A
knife rack in a drawer or on the kitchen wall will help to keep
the blades straight and undamaged. Use them only for the work
for which they were purchased not for odd jobs around the
house or garden.

Vegetable Knife A small knife with a short blade, 8-10 cms
long, which tapers to a point. A very useful knife for all small
preparation jobs such as peeling or preparing garnishes. A stainless steel vegetable knife with a serrated blade is useful for
cutting food which is difficult to slice neatly such as tomatoes
and oranges.

Filleting Knife This has a thin flexible blade about 18-20 ins long. Used for filleting fish and for boning and skinning both meat and fish.

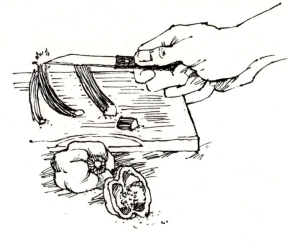

Cook's Knife A broad tapering bladed knife. The heel of the blade should be wider compared with the handle so that the fingers do not hit the table when using the knife for chopping. Use the knife with a wooden chopping board rather than a plastic surface. The hard plastic blunts the knife and because it is slippery, is not so easy to work on. These knives are obtainable with blades from 12-36 cms long but for most women the 12-18 cms sizes are the most comfortable to use.

Palette Knife or Spatula This has a round ended blade with no sharp edges. It is used for lifting and turning foods and for smoothing and finishing surfaces. It must be strong but flexible. The best material for a palette knife is carbon steel. Stainless is usually too flexible and is inclined to bend too much. The size of blade available ranges from 12-30 cms.

Potato Peeler There are so many different types of peeler available that it is a good idea to look at a number of them before making a final choice. You can buy peelers designed especially for use by left-handed people. A swivel bladed peeler allows you to pare the skin very finely.

Choppers and Cleavers These are a similar shape but the cleaver is slightly longer and deeper than the chopper. The blade is from 25-38 cms long. They are used for cutting bone and gristle and the back of the blade for cracking bones.

Freezer Knife and Meat Saw Particularly useful if you have a deep freezer. The meat saw is used for cutting through bone. It should not be used on fresh meat only on frozen meat. Freezer knives will cut through frozen food easily enabling you to cut up meat and poultry while it is still frozen and to cut large blocks of frozen fruit and vegetables into small neat portions.

Hachoir A crescent shaped chopping knife with a handle at each end. The single blade knife is the one most often used but it is possible to purchase two or four blade knives. Used for chopping up food finely. A small version complete with a wooden bowl is useful for chopping small quantities of herbs, onions or nuts.

Mandoline This is a rectangular frame fitted with cutting blades which can be set to slice vegetables and fruit to a desired thickness.

Spoons and Forks	
Basic 2 tablespoons 2 dessertspoons 2 teaspoons Wooden spoons of various sizes 2 table forks	*Non-essential* Perforated spoon 2-pronged cook's forks

Measuring Tools	

Basic
 	
 Measuring jug in liquid ounces and in metric measures
 Measuring spoons   table
                       tea
                       ½ tea
                       ¼ tea
 Measuring spoons in metric measures
	Non-essential
	
	 Scales with pounds and ounces and metric measures

Scales

These must be accurate. The balance type with weights is probably the more accurate and as there are no mechanical parts, more likely to remain so. The spring balance type, with a dial indicator of the weight, is quick and easy to use. The scales

should be strongly made of an easily cleaned material. The pan
should sit securely in position and be large enough to weigh the
quantities you are likely to need. In one model the pan is
shaped like a mixing bowl and it is intended for use as such.
After each ingredient to be mixed is added to the bowl the indicator can be set at zero ready for the next ingredient. Other
scales can be fitted to the wall and folded flat when not in use.
It is sensible to be able to weigh in pounds and ounces as well as
kilograms and grammes so that favourite recipes from old recipe
books can be used without having to make complicated
calculations.

Food Preparation	
Basic	*Non-essential*
Whisk	Mincing machine
Grater and shredder	Lemon squeezer
Tin opener	Flour dredger
Strainer	Funnel
Rolling pin	Pastry cutters—plain and fluted
Wire or nylon sieve	Wheeled pastry cutter
Corkscrew	Pastry board
Pastry brush	
Chopping board	
Kitchen scissors	

Whisks
1 Balloon whisk. This is supposed to be the only one able to
  beat egg whites to the correct consistency. Most people find
  it rather tiring to use. A small balloon whisk is useful for
  saucemaking and a large size for whisking cream and large
  quantities of egg white.
2 Rotary handwhisk. Choose one of stainless steel with nylon
  gears.
3 Circular coil of thick stainless steel wire fixed to a firm but
  flexible stainless steel wire handle. The efficiency of these
  depend on the size of the coil and the quality of the wire. It
  should be firm enough not to distort in use.
4 An electric whisk. (See 'Food Mixers')

Graters Different sized graters are needed for different foods, but several sizes may be incorporated into flat cylindrical and box type graters. Make sure you can hold the grater firmly and comfortably otherwise your hands will tire quickly. Mechanical graters with revolving drums are easy to use. A combined mincer/shredder/grater is available which is easy to assemble, use and clean.

Tin Openers should be able to open all types of tins with a clean, not jagged edge. The small rotating one is easier to use than the claw type which in any case cuts a jagged edge. A rotary opener which can be fitted to a small bracket on the wall is easy to use and can be folded away against the wall when not in use. It can be easily removed for cleaning. It may be fitted with a magnet which holds the lid as it is being cut off and prevents it falling into the tin.

Rolling Pins may be made of hardwood, glass, china, plastic or aluminium. They should be straight, smooth and reasonably heavy. Some are made with nonstick finishes which allow the pastry to be rolled using the minimum of flour. Others can be filled with cold water or ice cubes. Handle the rolling pin before you purchase it. Make sure the handles and the diameter of the pin are comfortable for you to use.

Kitchen Scissors Extra sharp kitchen scissors are almost indispensable for trimming meat and fish and cutting up herbs and garnishes. They can also act as nut crackers and bottle openers.

Mincing Machines These should be easily assembled and dismantled for cleaning. They should be in an easily cleaned material.

None of these are essential. You could do the work of each using a basic tool already mentioned in this chapter. However all these tools will do the work quickly and neatly. In each case check that the gadget is well made and will be able to do its job well for many years.

Spatula	Pestle and mortar
Fish slice	Bean slicer
Food tongs	Garlic crusher
Skewers	Egg slicer and segmenter
Potato masher	Cherry stoner
Nutcracker	Screw top opener
Butter curler	Potato chipper
Food Slicer	Steel cutters for potato and melon balls
Food Chopper	

Pots and Pans and Oven Ware	
Basic	*Non-essential*
Kettles—one small	One large kettle
Saucepans with lids—assorted sizes	Pan and basket for deep fat frying
	Fish kettle
Milk saucepan with lip or pouring rim	Preserving pan
Casseroles—assorted sizes	Omelette pan
Frying pan	Egg poacher

There is an almost bewildering choice of pots and pans to cook every type of food on every type of cooker. You can purchase these in many different shapes, materials, colours and prices. Nearly every one of these has something to commend it and something to limit its performance. The more you know about each type the easier you will find it to make up your mind what you need. Most homes have several different types according to the food to be cooked. This is usually more satisfactory than having a complete range of utensils made from one material.

You will already be quite familiar with a variety of different pans having used them at home or in school or in the homes of

friends and relatives. Unless they have been unusual or particularly attractive or difficult to clean the chances are that you have given them little attention. Start looking at them critically. Try to find out why a particular make or material was chosen. Note the items which are easily cleaned and those which take more time and effort. See if you can find the reason for the difference. Start taking notice of the different ranges shown in the shops and advertised in newspapers and magazines. Modern pots and pans are not the drab utilitarian utensils of even twenty years ago. They can now be a decorative feature to be taken into account when planning the kitchen and dining room. Compare them with the ones you can see in pictures, in your history books, in museums or even in kitchens equipped ten or fifteen years ago.

Here are some of the points you should consider when planning the purchase of these items:

1 The choice of materials. e.g. aluminium, enamel, stainless steel, copper, glass, tinned steel, cast iron.
2 Find out the ranges and sizes available. Collect and compare manufacturers advertisement leaflets. When you are first setting up your kitchen you will probably be able to manage with very basic items but you will soon want to add to these. It is a good idea to know just what is available.

3 The price range is very wide. If for some reason you only intend to keep the utensils for a very short time or use them infrequently you might be justified in buying cheap items. As a general rule this is not a good idea. Most people expect these utensils to last many years before needing replacement.

4 Bear in mind the type of fuel used for cooking (gas, electricity, oil or solid fuel) and whether the utensil is to be used in the oven or on the hob or both. Solid fuel or oil fired cookers and some electric hobs have solid plates. Heavy ground based pans must be used on these.

5 Investigate the ease of cleaning and the long term maintenance.

6 The heat conductibility. This will depend on the materials used to make the article. You must relate this to the speed you need to cook different foods, the means of cooking and the type of cooker.

7 Check the weight of the utensil. It should be light enough to use conveniently but heavy enough to prevent burning and if it is taken to the table, to retain heat.

8 The shape and colour should be appropriate to the use of the utensil. Lids should be well fitted so that steam and cooking smells cannot escape. Handles should be firmly fixed and comfortable to hold even when the utensil is full, heavy and hot. Frying pans, saucepans, and kettles should have heat resistant handles made of poor conductors of heat. Multi-purpose utensils such as oven to table ware and hob/oven/deep freeze ware sometimes have detachable handles. Test that these are quick and easy to take off and put on again without touching the hot pan and that they feel firm when attached. If they are to be used at table make sure they fit in with the colours and materials used there. Check the lip of pouring saucepans. If you are in doubt as to whether liquid can be poured easily and neatly ask the sales assistant for a demonstration. If this is refused do not purchase the saucepan. Look carefully at knobs, handle fixings, joins and decorative additions. Make sure there are no difficult to clean dirt traps. These are excellent breeding grounds for bacteria. Colours may be bright or subdued, plain or patterned.

9 Consider some of the modern ideas intended to save time or energy while cooking or washing up. Some are mere gim-

micks but others could be useful. Never buy a gadget of any sort if its assembly and cleaning uses more time and effort than its use saves.

Non-Stick Pots, Pans and Bakeware
The main considerations of the average homemaker when purchasing cookware are that it should be easy to clean, light in weight and heat evenly over the whole base. These properties are regarded as more important than good looks or durability. Few people would tolerate having to spend hours scouring heavy pots and pans as our ancestors were forced to do.

In addition to all the innovations which have enabled us to have attractive, strong and easily cared for cooking pans we can now purchase pans which have a non-stick coating inside. More than two thirds of the households in Great Britain have one or two of these pans in use and the numbers are steadily increasing.

The basic material used for the finish is a slippery heat-resistant plastic called polytetrafluoroethylene (PTFE). It is resistant to chemical and high temperatures. Because PTFE is a relatively soft material it scratches easily and as a result wooden spatulas had to be used to avoid damaging the surface. In 1970 manufacturers started producing a scratch resistant non-stick finish on a hard base.

1 The metal pan is first cleaned completely free of grease
2 The surface is grit blasted and all the dust is removed
3 A hard base of a ceramic grit is sprayed on in molten form 4
4 A primer coat is applied and air-dried or baked onto the surface
5 A top coat of PTFE containing colouring pigment, usually black, is applied and fused on at a temperature of 440°C

This non-stick surface is being used for many household appliances besides pots and pans, bakeware and oven ware. These include food slicers, kitchen knives, waffle irons, coffee makers, irons and automatic egg cookers, rolling pins, steak grills, and cream whippers. Non-stick appliances will last longer and give more efficient service if you follow the manufacturers instructions for use and care.

Cleaning PTFE Coated Appliances

This is very easy to do. After each use any PTFE coated appliance should be thoroughly cleaned with a sponge or soft dish cloth or mop in hot water with detergent. It is not sufficient to wipe it over with a damp cloth or to give it a brief rinse under the tap. Even if it appears clean after this treatment a film of food could be left on the surface. If this built up with each use and finally carbonised the pan would become sticky and appear to lose its non-stick surface.

Metal scourers and scouring powders should never be used. If food appears to be burnt on, a short soak in cold water and detergent will loosen it, or as a final resort a rubber scraper or a plastic mesh pad may be used.

The brown stain which sometimes forms on non-stick pans can be removed with a solution of a cup of hot water to a half a cup of liquid chlorine bleach and 2 tablespoons of sodium bicarbonate. This should be brought to the boil in the stained pan and then simmered for 10 minutes. Empty the pan and scrub it with a nylon brush or pad and then wash it thoroughly.

Kitchen China	
Basic	*Non-essential*
Mixing bowls	Jelly moulds
3 or 4 pudding basins various sizes	Souffle dishes
Casseroles	
Pie dishes	
Pie plate	
Plates	
Jugs	

All these items can be purchased in a number of sizes. Start off with the most useful sizes for everyday use. You can add other sizes as the need arises or as you can afford them.

Casseroles, Pie Dishes and Souffle Dishes can be purchased to match tableware.

Most Kitchen China and Glass can be purchased in colours and patterns as well as in plain white china and clear heat resistant glass.

Baking and Cake tins	
Basic	*Non-essential*
Set of bun tins	Boat shaped tins
2 Sandwich tins	Cream horn tins
2 Cake tins (15 and 20 cms diameter)	Dariole moulds
Baking sheet or swiss roll tin	Flan rings—plain and fluted
Wire cake rack	Bread tins
Meat tins	Angel cake tins
	Larger and smaller round cake tin
	Set of square cake tins

Whenever possible choose tins with easy care non-stick finishes. This will save time by not having to line the tins and by the ease with which they can be washed. These are utensils bought to last so get the best quality you can afford.

Bun Tins Choose tins with deep shapes. The shallow tins produce tartlets with little space for the jam and flat buns which tend to be dry because of the amount of outer crust compared with its size.

Cake Tins Tins with removable bases are useful.

Cake Decoration	
Basic	*Non-essential*
Icing pipes, plain and rose	Large, medium and small forcing bags
Meringue plain and rose	Marking rings
Greaseproof paper to make bags	Wider range of pipes
Adapter	Turntable
Fine mesh sieve	Nails

Most women find it easier to use a pipe and bag rather than a cumbersome icing set. A far more professional finish can be obtained with these.

Pipes Stainless steel pipes give a finer edge to the piping but inexpensive plastic pipes are quite suitable for everyday use. Should you intend to do more advanced work it is well worth while investing in a set of stainless steel pipes.

Forcing bags You can purchase proofed nylon bags for icing and piping potatoes in several sizes. If they are used properly and washed and dried according to the maker's instructions they should give many years wear. Icing bags of greaseproof paper are easily made and can be discarded after use.

Adapter This is put into the mouth of the forcing bag. It enables you to change pipes without emptying the bag.

Marking Rings These simplify the marking out of a cake. The rings themselves are marked into divisions.

Turntable The ideal turntable is of heavy weight, easily cleaned, metal which can be revolved easily even when a really large cake is on it. Designed for professional use it should last a lifetime in the home. A popular model made of lightweight metal will wear quite well if you take care that it is washed and dried very carefully after use and not allowed to rust.

A lazy Susan tray of laminated plastic can serve as an icing turntable if it is raised by resting it on a large tin or an up-turned drawer of the required height. It is fairly easy to adapt the turntable of a discarded record player or gramophone to serve the same purpose.

Food Containers

There is an unlimited choice of food containers on the market made of materials such as glass, plastic and pottery. They can cost very little or be really luxurious in elegant matched sets. Whatever the type you choose it is important that they should be dust, damp and insect proof. If you have little money to spare for specially designed containers collect the screw topped jars in which various foods are sold. Some products are sold in different sizes so that you can get jars small enough for herbs or long enough for sugar and flour. Paint the lids in bright colours to tone in with the colour scheme of your kitchen. Make sure all containers are neatly and clearly labelled..